MANLY ADVENTURES II
AND OTHER DELUSIONS:

Sudden Impact

BY TOM WILSON
ILLUSTRATED BY DANNY SHAW

RED APPLE PUBLISHING

LIBRARY OF CONGRESS CATALOG CARD NUMBER 98-68706

ISBN 1-880222-31-0

● RED APPLE PUBLISHING
PEGGY MEYER, EDITOR/PUBLISHER
15010 113TH ST. KPN
GIG HARBOR, WA 98329-5014

PAGE AND COVER DESIGN BY KATHY CAMPBELL

PRINTED BY GORHAM PRINTING
ROCHESTER, WA 98579-8920

MANUFACTURED IN THE UNITED STATES OF AMERICA

IN MEMORY OF

Patrick Boyle & Theodore Shaw, Sr.

DEDICATED TO

Ma & Pa T (Micki & Harold Tassin)

Contents

Das Boat Buck

FRIEND DALE LIVES ON THE PUGET SOUND, BOATING CAPITAL of the entire world. This area has more boats per capita than some places have kids per capita. There are race boats and row boats, whale boats and sail boats, little boats, big boats, wide boats and skinny boats.

Dale has dreamed his entire life that one day he would own a yacht. He would stand proud and straight on the flying bridge, wind blowing through his hair. Twin gas engines, powerful and manly, would roar beneath his feet. He'd be Captain of his fate—Master of his destiny. He would cruise past small fishing boats, nose in the air, and scoff at their insignificance as they struggled to stay afloat in his powerful wake.

He would speed past sail boats on windless days and snicker at their stupidity. "Those sailboat people are a strange lot anyway," he would say. "They are always too busy with their ropes and their deck shoes to properly scoff at anyone, and they never seem to be sure of where they are going—first they go left—then they go right—then they go left again."

Time had finally come for action. Dale had saved some money and, after liquidating all of his worldly assets and

signing three pounds of papers for a sizable loan, he paid cash for his first yacht. I was honored to be offered a tour of his new vessel and I accepted his invitation to accompany him on the inaugural cruise. Maybe I too will buy a yacht, I thought.

"This here is my baby," Dale chortled, grinning from ear to ear. "Forty foot of fabulous fiberglass!"

"Pretty cool," I said. "How do I get on?"

"There's a ladder on the stern."

"Okay! I, ah, is that the pointy end or the flat-lookin' end?"

I took the complete tour.

"Well," he proudly smirked. "Whatcha think?"

"I really like it, but . . ."

"But what?"

"But I bumped my head on the ceiling when I walked through the door to the bedroom, and there appears to be a deep scratch on the left side of the front end."

Dale quickly informed me that I had bumped my head on the overhead as I went through the hatch into the stateroom and that he had already noticed, thank you very much, the scratch on the port side of the bow.

Pretty cool terminology. Once again I thought maybe I too will buy a yacht.

"So, Captain, ah, what do I get to be?"

"You can be my deck hand."

"I ain't being nobody's deck hand!"

"Okay! Then how about Executive Officer?"

"That sounds pretty cool," I said, chest slightly puffing. "What does the Executive Officer do?"

"Pretty much deck-hand stuff . . . but I promise to respect you a lot more!"

Dale fired up the engines. I'm here to tell ya that the roar of those babies was pretty manly, and I was startin' to have multiple thoughts about gettin' one of these yachts.

"Sounds pretty meaty!" I yelled. "Does she use a lot a gas?"

"No!" Dale yelled back. "I won't miss mowing my grass!"

"No! I said GAS. Does she use a LOT OF GAS?"

Dale backed off on the throttle. "Well, it depends. If ya keep her down around 8 or 9 knots, she'll burn about a gallon a mile. But if ya kick her up to 23 knots, she'll suck up about thirty gallons an hour."

"Thirty gallons a what?" I stuttered.

"An hour," he said somewhat proudly.

"So let's see. If ya go one hundred miles at 23 knots," I calculated out loud, "she'll suck up around one hundred and twenty gallons of gas at a buck fifty per gallon. Is that about right?"

"Yup!"

Ouch, maybe I might get me a smaller yacht.

"What?"

"I said that seems like a lot!"

"Well, yeah, but it sure is worth it."

"So, ah, does the Executive Officer have to pay for any of that gas? I mean you were gonna go out for a cruise today anyway, right?"

Dale told me to just relax while he piloted the boat out of the slip.

"Is it easy to back her out?" I asked.

"Well, the rudder doesn't work till you're up to speed, so ya gotta use the two engines like thrusters to start, stop, and change direction. It's kinda like trying to parallel park a forty-foot car in a patch of ice with a blindfold on."

"So, ah, Captain Dale, you thought of a name for her yet?"

"Yup, Umiak. I'm gonna call her the Umiak."

"Oh!"

"Whaddahya mean OH! You gotta problem with Umiak?"

"No, I don't have a problem with Umiak. I was just wondering what an Umiak might be. Is that like a giant, dog-eating frog or something?"

"An Umiak is a small, hand-made, wooden boat made by the natives in Alaska."

"Oh, well, that explains the fiberglass," I sarcastically mumbled.

"What?"

"I said that name has a lot of class." When I get me a boat, I'm gonna name it something simple like maybe Tom's Boat.

As I looked toward the pointy end, I noticed a strange object sitting on the dock.

"So, ah, what's that rusty old tank lookin' thing sitting over there?"

"That's the old, steel, water heater. It rusted clean through so I bought a new stainless steel one."

"What did that set ya back?"

"I got her for two and a half boat bucks."

"Oh," I said, "and what's a boat buck?"

Dale proceeded to explain that, unlike regular bucks that are worth around thirty-five cents each, a boat buck is variable, seasonal, completely unassociated with any known economic indicators such as reality, and usually runs between twenty and one-hundred regular bucks. He told numerous stories of shopping at the local hardware store and paying about $1.79 for a quart of vinyl paint, or two feet of rubber hose, or one NGK-45 spark plug, or four wire brushes. At the local boat store, he explained, you would pay anywhere from $4.79 to $9.95 for the very same items. I asked him how they could possibly stay in business by so blatantly ripping off the educated boating public.

"They put the word *Marine* on every item," he explained. "It's kinda like being blessed."

Dale masterfully coerced her out of the parking spot and headed for open water on the inaugural cruise. I manned my position on the pointy end and did Executive Officer stuff. I gazed down at the water as it boiled under the boat at an amazing speed of about a boat buck a mile and contemplated all that I had learned. Maybe, I mumbled out loud, I should buy a small, aluminum, fishing boat.

We cruised under the steel bridge and headed into the channel.

"Looks like fog ahead, Captain!" I shouted. "Maybe we should turn the pointy end around and head back to the dock."

"Don't worry about it," Dale beamed. "I have radar, a Global Positioning Satellite thing, and a compass."

"I'll bet ya that cost ya a couple a dozen boat bucks," I mumbled.

"What did you say?"

"I said I once got lost in the fog with my cousin in a goat truck!"

"Oh, well, don't worry. We'll be fine."

I find it hard to believe just how lost you can get when

you can't see where you are. Fortunately, I knew that the Captain and his toys would guide us to safety.

"So, Captain, did you hear that horn over there?"

"Yeah, I heard it. I think it's the car ferry."

"Whaddahya mean you think it's the car ferry! Ya mean you're not sure?"

"Don't get excited, man. I'm pretty sure it's the car ferry."

"Whaddahya mean don't get excited? Whaddahya mean you're pretty sure? That thing will squash us! Look on the radar and see if you can spot it!"

"Okay, okay! Get out the book on the radar and see if you can figure out how to operate it."

"What! Whaddahya mean get out the stupid radar book? The ferry will kill us before I get to the second paragraph. Fire up that stupid Global Positioning thing and get us outta here!"

"Well, I, ah, can't use the GPS cause you can't tell it where to go if you don't know where you are. I mean you can put in the coordinates of where you want to be but you might cruise through a land mass on the way there."

"Oh, Lord, forgive me for I have sinned."

The car ferry sound was getting louder. You could feel the vibrations of its massive engines.

"Okay, look," I reasoned. "We were going east when we left. If we just head west on the compass, we should end up back at the dock."

Dale didn't respond.

"Captain!" I screamed. "What does the compass say?"

"I think the compass is broke. It says we're headed south, but that's impossible because just a few minutes ago it showed us heading north. And I'm pretty sure we're headed east right now."

Why is the compass always broke when you get lost in the fog!

The car ferry suddenly became visible. As it roared past us fewer than fifty feet away, I could see the passengers lined up on the deck, noses in the air, scoffing at our insignificance as we struggled to stay afloat in their powerful wake.

I've decided that what I really need is a small, red, eight-foot rowboat. That should run me about two boat bucks!

Aerobiphobia

I REALLY DON'T KNOW WHY SHE ASKED. I WAS LYING BACK IN my recliner, minding my own business, scratching the gently curved portion of my belly, and channel surfing like I do every night. She walked over and stood right in front of my football game.

"Dear," she said, kicking the foot stool of my chair, "why don't you come to aerobics with me tonight and give it a try?"

"Aerobics!" I stammered. "That's not for men. That's girl stuff!"

"Yes, dear," she curtly replied. "A real man would surely turn to mush if he did aerobics, but in your case your body has already pretty much achieved optimum mushness—so the damage should be minimal. Besides, it would be nice if you got up out of that stupid chair and let some blood flow to your big butt."

It was apparent that the woman really didn't understand. A man's body is a finely tuned machine with powerful leg muscles and strong, sinewy arms. A real man tears ugly, vicious, evil-tempered beasts into tiny, harmless, insignificant pieces of animal flesh seconds before they pounce on and devour young, beautiful, nubile, helpless, blond-haired

women. A real man must hunt, fish, and participate in contact sports to truly maintain his manly physique.

She was, as always, persistent. "Please, my pet," she sarcastically pleaded, "pretty please with sugar on it, go with me to aerobics . . . or completely forget about getting any dinner tonight."

Hey, what could I do? It was either say yes or spend thirty minutes listening to that *pretty please with sugar on it* garbage, followed by three or four days of eating canned chili. I couldn't let the little woman down. Besides, it might be entertaining to watch a bunch of gals wearing multicolored, brightly flowered, skin-tight, stretch pants jumpin' up 'n' down making fools of themselves.

"Okay, ladies," the instructor boomed, "let's form our lines for stretching." I found myself a good viewpoint on the bleachers as the gals lined up in neat little rows for warm-up exercises. I couldn't help but notice that the instructor kept looking in my direction. She was in her mid-twenties and in fine shape. Obviously, I thought to myself, she finds me irresistible. I sucked in my gut and gave her a little wink.

"Is something wrong with your eye?" my wife yelled.

"No, my sweetness," I shot back defiantly, "just an eyelash, dear."

The instructor smiled and pointed her finger at me.

"Would you like to join in?" she yelled.

I looked to both sides of the empty bench and stuck my right index finger in the middle of my chest.

"Who, me?" I stuttered.

"Yes, you," she challenged. "We would all enjoy the company of a real man."

There was something eerie about the cumulative sound of a room full of snickering women that made me just a wee bit nervous. My lovely wife was doing an excellent job of cupping her hand over her mouth to muffle her outburst of rapturous laughter.

"No thanks," I stammered. "I'm in pretty good shape. I think I'll just watch."

"It's probably just as well," she countered. "It's unlikely you could keep up anyway."

I find it astounding how fragile manliness can be. One well-timed, derisive criticism from virtually any female can instantaneously peel away the delicate facade of any man's manliness.

Several women were now crossing their legs to keep from peeing while laughing hysterically. There was nothing more to say. I had just been subjected to the laying of the gauntlet. The kid gloves had been slapped across my cheek. The line had been drawn in the sand with a high heel. The rice cake had been flicked from my shoulder.

The testosterone surged in my veins. I was driven from the bleachers and down to an empty spot on the hardwood floor next to my wife. The instructor just smiled.

"Okay, girls," she commanded. "It's time. Let's get started. March in place now—left and right and left and right . . . "

Oh, this is really tough, I chuckled to myself. I'll just teach these gals how it should really be done by showing 'em up with a little military double time. Lef-right-lef-right-lef-right . . .

"Slow down, you idiot," my wife demanded. "If you strain yourself, you're gonna have to hire someone to feel sorry for ya."

"Ha!" I confidently replied. I could march in step for hours and not even break a sweat.

"When do they get to the hard stuff?"

I still, to this very day, don't know exactly what happened. I can vaguely remember doing some kinda country-line-dance routine and then stepping up and down on some wooden block. I remember being confused as to why I was flat on my back looking up at the ceiling, surrounded by a whole tribe of multicolored, brightly flowered, skin-tight, stretch pants. I can still hear the sweet voice of my loving wife offering her support and encouragement as I lay in a breathless heap on the floor.

"Dear, you appear to be panting like a dog. It's quite becoming."

I remember trying to focus on the face of a large, greasy, red-headed woman who was pinching my nose with the gnarled fingers of her left hand while blowing garlic-tainted puffs of air into my lifeless lungs.

I can only conclude that this aerobic business is a plot perpetrated by some feminist female doctor to utilize girl muscles and render permanent physiological damage to the unsuspecting male of the species.

Chair Man

IT IS MID-NOVEMBER. I AM SITTING IN MY CHAIR. MY WIFE Lynne will quickly tell you that my chair is not my chair. She will explain in great detail how we purchased the chair together and that the chair is *our* chair and most definitely not *my* chair. I'm here to tell you that the chair is my chair. When I'm tired, worn down and depressed from a hard, tedious day of manly adventures, I take great solace in knowing that my chair will be there when I get home.

My father had a chair, my grandfather had a chair, and my great-grandfather had a chair. For thousands of years the men of my family, and most likely the men of your family, lay claim to only one true possession—their chair. My earliest recorded Neanderthal ancestor, Mot, would sit in his hand-carved rock chair and cook meat on a fire. The cave, the authentic wall scratchings, the geologically functional lava lamp, the clay pottery, the bed of leaves, and the entire collection of sun-dried animal skins all belonged to Ennyl, wife of Mot . . . . Rock chair belong to Mot.

In the spring of 1886, the revered British archeologist, Sir Phillip Crane, discovered the mummified remains of Mot during an exploratory dig deep in the hidden caves of Madagascar.

Mot was found hunched over, yet still sitting, in the crumbled remains of his rock chair. Sir Crane reported in his memoirs that an unmistakable smile was frozen on the face of Mot's wrinkled corpse.

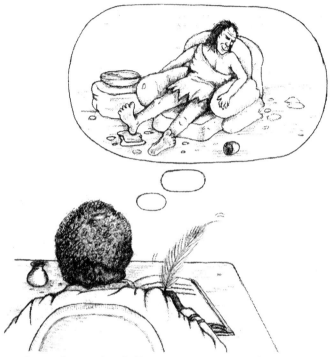

Throughout the following centuries, from generation to generation, the seed of Mot would solidify its historical hierarchy in the annals of time. The prodigies of Mot were both weak and powerful. Their accomplishments were both great and insignificant, and yet there is one common thread that bonds the generations in their manliness. Therefore I say unto you: You can wash the dishes, hold her purse in the store, fold all the laundry and wax the darn floor. You can do all these things without splitting a hair if you're one of the manly men who has his own chair.

Cabo

I JUST GOT BACK FROM CABO SAN LUCAS ON THE TIP OF BAJA—
a virtual paradise in the Mexican desert. A large rock forma-
tion protrudes from west of downtown Cabo and serves as
the southern-most point of the Baja Peninsula. On one side of
the rock lies the Pacific Ocean and on the other side the Sea of
Cortez.

The sun rises early each morning and paints the ocean
waters with a sparkling display of yellow and orange lumines-
cence. The warm ocean breezes caress the tourists as they
lounge by the heated pool drinking cool margaritas. The com-
fort of dawn blends quickly into the glowing warmth of mid-
morning as children splash and squeal with delight.

Around noon, as the sun rises high in the sky and the
breeze stills, the mercury bursts from the tops of thermom-
eters. The lounge chairs empty of the sunburned bodies of
overweight Caucasians while small children scream in pain as
their tiny bare feet touch the iron-hot surfaces of the brick
courtyard. Hell's fire hath come to God's country.

Fortunately, one can catch an air-conditioned Volkswagen
bus to beautiful downtown Cabo. There, on the crumbling, filthy,
uneven, handlaid, red-brick walkways, you find yourself under

siege from an army of relentless, timeshare mercenaries. Small children in tattered clothing line the roadway tugging at your leg. They stare up at you with sunken little eyes and plead for you to buy their five-cent, stale candies for two dollars. You escape by ducking into one of the many fine restaurants that dot the main street.

The food is marvelous. The fish is freshly caught and hand dipped in rich Mexican herbs and spices. The vegetables are steamed or broiled to perfection. If you're observant, you can see the bore holes of plant-eating insects prominently displayed on the outside surfaces of your carrots. Please note that the food poisoning that afflicted me seldom targets young children, though the few rare exceptions have resulted in painful and instantaneous death.

The evening hours offer a return of the ocean breezes that serve to once again cool the sting of the relentless solar fireball. Many tourists, finding the hotel swimming pools much too crowded and noisy, head for the blue ocean waters. The beaches are mile after mile of beautiful, fine, white sand. The rolling, bath-like temperature of the surf caresses the shoreline with a gentle tumbling thunder that instantly sucks small children out to sea and into the waiting mouths of the thousands of deep-sea, salt-water predators that ply the waters in a perpetual feeding frenzy.

Many parents refuse to allow their young children to play in the surf, claiming it is too dangerous. They opt instead for the apparent relative safety of the hotel recreation area and swimming pool, virtually ignoring the hundreds of poisonous snakes and scorpions that cross the highway from the desert

and wander hungrily around the landscaped hotel grounds.

For sports enthusiasts, the twenty miles of paved roads are home to a dozen world-class golf courses. I'm not a player myself, but I understand you can buy a round of something and get some kinda green fee for just shy of one hundred and fifty dollars. That certainly sounds like a good deal to me!

I would like to thank each of you for giving me this opportunity to share my vacation experience. I had a great time in Cabo and I hope that all of you take advantage of the reasonable cost of air fare and hotel accommodations and share this piece of tropical paradise. As for the persistent rumors that roving gangs of Mexican Banditos swoop down from the mountains and snatch nubile, young women away from their boyfriends, you couldn't prove it by me!

Sudden Impact

IT WAS FRIDAY, 4:20 P.M. WE'RE TALKING "END OF THE WORK-week" here. My true friend and supportive buddy Dale and I headed out the front door of the building where we both work and crossed the street heading home. The early summer sun was warm on our faces, and a gentle breeze was blowing from the east. This was going to be a glorious weekend.

"Hey, look at this clown," Dale observed. "He's driving before the whistle!"

I looked over my right shoulder and saw a gray van heading east toward the exit gate. This is a definite *no no.* I work in a large industrial complex. Access to the worksite is secured, and identification badges are worn while on the premises. A standing rule, for the sake of safety, dictates that only pedestrian traffic is allowed for the first seven minutes of the commute. This guy was three minutes shy of being legal. I continued walking while waving my right hand at the offender— trying to attract his attention. What I attracted was an eight-foot-high signpost!

The post was metallic and approximately two-and-one-half inches in diameter. Its external radius matched precisely the contour formed by the right side of my nose—where it used to gently blend into my cheekbone. I find it amazing that a warm-blooded mass of flesh traveling at approximately three miles per hour could suffer such a debilitating impact from the unexpected and abrupt termination of forward progress caused by encountering a stationary, inanimate object. The post did not move from its true position—though witnesses reported afterward that the impact caused slight vibrations to undulate upward from the impact zone. The rigidity of my proboscis was, however, temporarily compromised by the resulting multiple fractures. The ridge that runs from between your eyes to the tip of your nose is called the septum—which was now deviated from its genetically intended location.

I remember being stunned. I would expound on *stunned* but I was so stunned that I can't recall anything except being stunned. I know I personally saw four or five previously uncharted galaxies, and I was later told that I did the Texas-two-step into an untrimmed thorn bush that adorned the side of the walkway.

I have never seen blood wait so long to come out. It must have been almost twenty seconds after impact when a torrential downpour of hemoglobin suddenly flowed from my right nostril. I held my hand over the rushing torrent, but, as you can imagine, the left side of my right thumb had little chance of absorbing anything.

"Help me!" I pleaded. "I'm gonna bleed to death here!"

My friend Dale quickly rallied in support—along with Ron and Jack who joined Dale at my side.

Dale was first to speak. "What happened?"

I explained, with an annoying nasal buzz, that I had walked into the signpost and broke my nose and that, at the moment, I appeared to be basically bleeding to death. He offered immediate encouragement, "You mean I missed the whole darn thing?" he stammered. "I can't believe I was walking right next to you and I missed the whole darn thing."

"I saw it," said Jack. "It was pretty cool."

"Excuse me," I begged. "Would someone please give me a Kleenex or a corner of your shirt or something. I'm really worried about . . ."

Jack or Ron interrupted, "Did you see it when the pole vibrated? It was impressive! I don't think I have ever seen anybody stop that fast in my entire life?"

Dale was apparently stuck in a state of disappointed redundancy. "I can't believe I was walking right next to him and I missed the whole thing!" he repeated.

"Excuse me, pals," I gurgled. "I'm, ah, getting faint here. I could really use some basic first-aid before I pass out."

Ron handed me his handkerchief—which I placed over my right nostril. I applied a great deal of direct pressure. Liquid, they tell me, will seek the route of least resistance. With the primary exit hole plugged, I began to spit copious amounts of biohazard onto the sidewalk. But, I managed to make it to my car.

I drove all of the way home with that handkerchief

pressed tightly in place. I worried about whether or not Ron had given me an expensive handkerchief and if I would have to replace it. After an hour the bleeding finally stopped. I removed the cloth which was tie-dyed a vibrant red. I could see that it was a cheap hanky so replacement was not a concern. I also noticed that it had not been recently laundered as it was encrusted with large slabs of dried nasal excretion that unfortunately belonged to the original owner. Yuck!

My wife insisted that I get to the Emergency Care Center. The eye, nose, ear and throat guy checked out my nasal airways and pronounced them clear. He told me that my nose was slightly bent to one side. He said it looked good on me.

The next day a friend at work, Gloria, mentioned that I should follow my nose even if I do end up walking around in circles. Empathy appears to be a lost art. Had the whole incident been filmed, I could send it to the Funniest Home Video show on TV. I'm sure it would fit in perfectly with the other really funny clips of people getting seriously injured while their friends laugh hysterically!

My five-year-old told me I looked like a unicorn.

My wife provided my only solace. She insisted that I not worry about how my nose looked. She assured me that most people would not even notice that I now appeared twisted and disfigured.

I find it astounding how fragile manliness can be. One well-timed, derisive criticism from virtually any female can instantaneously peel away the delicate facade of any man's manliness.

Her heartless comments actually left me emotionally

wounded and wallowing in some serious self-doubt. The next day I sent an e-mail to her place of employment in search of reassurance. I asked her if she was going to trade me in because my nose was hooked and knurly. When I received no response, I called her on the phone.

"Dear," I whimpered, "I sent you an e-mail this morning asking if you were gonna trade me in. It's past two o'clock and I haven't heard a word from you. Why didn't you return my message? Are you embarrassed to be seen communicating with the Elephant Man?"

"I saw your e-mail message," she impatiently explained, "but they took my lap-top away to update some programs and I haven't had a chance to respond."

"So, can you send me an e-mail now?" I pleaded.

"I can't send you an e-mail right now," she whispered. "I have important people in my office."

"Oh," I mumbled, somewhat disappointed. "Then can you tell me over the phone whether or not you want to trade me in?"

"Okay, okay! I might as well get it over with," she groaned. "No, I'm not going to trade you in. There, now do you feel better?"

"Because you really do love me?" I said, perking up.

"No," she snapped, "because with a nose like that nobody would give me anything for you!"

Butt Out

I DON'T REMEMBER WHEN IT HAPPENED, SOMETIME IN THE '80s I think. Women started talking out loud, in public, about men's butts. I'm sure they have always thought about men's butts, but this talking out loud about men's butts thing just seemed to happen. I can't go anywhere without having to listen to a bunch of cackling women talk about some poor man's butt. We have minds too, ya know. They talk about movie stars' butts and rock stars' butts. They brag about their boyfriend's butt, or they giggle over their girlfriends' boyfriends' butts. They watch highly skilled, finely tuned Olympic athletes who have spent almost their entire lives preparing for one shot at a world record and a gold medal, and all they can do is talk about their butts!

I mean I'm sick of it. Every man I know is sick of it. I am really, really tired of hearing about Kevin Costner's butt. He makes an epic, three-hour Western about the life and times of the Plains Indians and all they talk about is the butt scene. Besides, I heard that he had a butt stand-in. I like Mel Gibson's *Lethal Weapon* movies—the action, the thrills. What do you suppose the wife and daughter talk about? The bomb in the bathroom scene? The highway chase with the armored car? The bullet-riddled trailer? The suicide attempt on the sky-scraper? No! They talk about Mel's butt! Why the hell does Hollywood even bother writing a screen play? Why don't they just hire Costner and Gibson to make a three-hour movie of their butts! The gross proceeds from my house alone would offset production costs!

Seriously, I am very concerned about this butt thing. I have been trying on jeans in the changing room at the Mall and I have actually seen, with my own two eyes, grown men standing with their backs to the mirror, looking over their shoulders at their butts! Everywhere you look it's happening.

There are women where I work who vote on which male coworker has the nicest butt. I just know a bunch a' women got together and invented spandex bicycle shorts. Let's face it, this is some kinda sick thing that's happening here. I used to go to the local pub with the boys, have a brew or two, and watch an occasional wet tee-shirt or prettiest barmaid competition. Now you're liable to walk in on some stupid Men's Butt Night.

I have even started being sensitive about my own butt. I stay up nights wondering if my butt's too small or too flat or too flabby.

I never used to worry about my butt. Now, when I go shopping for pants, I don't know if I should buy tight pants to show off my butt or loose pants to hide it. On several occasions I have made the mistake of asking my wife about my butt. She once told me that ever since I hit forty I had a better butt in the front than I did in the back. She usually says something like, "Yes, my pet, you have a very nice butt." And then she goes back to watching some Mel Gibson movie for the fifteenth time. My very own loving daughter, the one whom I raised with my own two hands, tells me that I don't have a butt. She says the only butt I have is my wallet. Maybe I should get two wallets and even my butt out. Maybe I should start padding my wallets. I wonder if you can get silicon wallet implants. What the heck is my seventeen-year-old daughter doing looking at my butt anyway? Can you get a butt lift? Are they expensive? Would they put the scar where you couldn't tell, kind of a tuck 'n' roll?

Next thing ya know they're gonna come out with special stuff for men's butts—Butt lotion, Wonder Butt bra's. How about stuff to pamper the functioning part of our butt—like manly toilet paper imprinted with fish or wild animals or sports stars or something. Maybe a famous skier doing a wipe out.

I digress. The point is, men, it's time we get off our butts, quit assing out, and face this thing head on or we will forevermore be relegated to bringing up the rear.

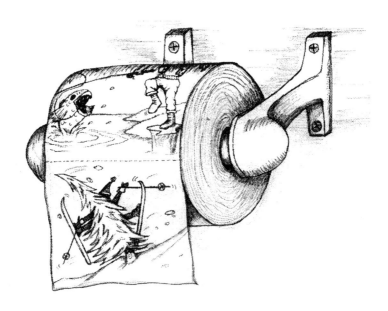

The Karate Kid

JOHN GREW UP ON THE ISLAND OF GUAM. HE HAS NUMEROUS stories to tell of his wild and reckless youth. John and his friends were a manly group of teens. They had studied karate and had formed a karate club. They considered themselves the toughest dudes on the island. The island residents considered them bullies. Though the philosophy of karate embraces the art of self-defense, Saturday nights would find the boys cruising the island in search of hapless victims. There were few locals who would challenge their skills and even fewer who could hold their own against the unmerciful onslaught.

John remembers the feeling of frustration when there seemed to be no challengers left on the island that were worthy of their superior karate skills. One day word came that the Japanese Olympic Karate Team was visiting the island. They were to give a karate exhibition at the local gym. John and the rest of his club made plans to be there. They were not prepared for what they found.

The announcer explained to the crowd that the Japanese demonstration would be a no contact drill. The boys laughed at the concept. What kind of babies would show off their karate skills without even touching their opponents. The boys walked out of the exhibition before it started.

They left a very rude message for the visitors—challenging the Japanese team to a real, full-contact match, unless of course they were afraid. The Japanese team sent word back to John and the boys that their challenge was honorably accepted. The match was set for the next day in the gym. The Japanese team insisted on two conditions: (1) the contest was to be advertised and open to the public, and (2) donations would be contributed to local charities.

The gym filled with spectators. The boys were excited by the opportunity to display their prowess against an Olympic opponent. John was the first competitor to walk out on the mat. The partisan crowd chanted his name: John! John! John! John! John! His opponent walked out on the mat and stood facing him. The Japanese boy bowed. John turned to look at his teammates, shrugged his shoulders, and laughed. He assumed that there must have been a mistake. He was facing an opponent who was clearly a wimp. The Japanese athlete was a tiny, delicate, manicured, pedicured, slightly effeminate boy with short, perfectly trimmed, black hair. John planned to show little mercy. He would make short work of this girlie man, return to the bench, and enjoy the remainder of the match.

The signal was given to begin. John had a special hold he had worked on for years to perfect. He grabbed the delicate little Japanese boy by his lapel, jumped up in the air, and planted his right foot firmly in his opponent's chest. Once in this position his opponent would be helpless and could be

quickly flipped to the floor. John can't recall exactly how he himself ended up twisted in half and slammed to the mat. It all happened too fast. He only remembers looking up into his opponent's eyes. The Japanese boy had a solid grip on John's left wrist, his right foot was planted firmly in John's armpit, and John's arm was twisted about seventeen degrees beyond design specifications.

The Japanese boy smiled down at John and then looked over to the Japanese bench for a signal from the coach. The coach stood with his feet apart, arms folded across his chest. He held out his right arm, extended his thumb, and pointed it at the floor. The message was clear. There was a rapid twist, followed by a dull pop, and John's arm—no longer hinged to the torso—was released. It fell limp and numb to the mat.

John stressed later that the popping sound was not representative of the actual physical feeling associated with having your arm dislocated at the shoulder, though he was unable to provide a word, or words, that he considered appropriate to describe the resulting excruciating pain.

The Japanese boy quickly switched to John's right wrist. John offered no resistance other than a slightly inaudible whimper. The left foot was planted firmly in John's armpit, and the Japanese boy once again smiled. The coach stood firm, arms still folded across his chest. He held out both arms, extended both thumbs, and pointed them at the floor. The Japanese boy, apparently accomplishing the instructional portion of the event, performed several simultaneous gyrations in slow motion. There were actually three audible pops as opposed to the one dull pop that occurred when the maneuver was accomplished at regular speed.

The little Japanese boy methodically moved to John's legs. He popped the right leg and finished with a solid popping of the left leg. Contrary to crowd expectations, and no doubt due to anatomical differences, the leg pops were actually quieter than the arm pops. Each movement was preceded by a sadistic thumbs-down signal from the Japanese coach. John's dysfunctional body was dragged to the side of the mat and

dropped in a contorted position in front of John's teammates. He was left there moaning and shaking, unable to speak.

Rumor has it that the one-sided match continued for over an hour, though there was minimal enthusiasm from the remainder of the Guamanian karate team. The results were embarrassingly similar, though the adverse treatment of John apparently sufficed as an adequate example and there were no more dislocations. John was left in a lump alongside the mat for the duration, and he reportedly retired from karate the very next day. Word has it he can tell you when the weather is going to change a good twenty-four hours in advance.

For Pete's Sake

THEY HAD TRAVELED FOR HOURS TO REACH THIS ISOLATED SPOT in the dark, moist, rain forest of the Pacific Northwest. Pete and Margaret were exhausted from the long journey. She leaned her head on her husband's shoulder and they were silent. The sounds of the wilderness stirred the pioneer spirit in Pete. This, he thought to himself, is *man country.*

"Listen, Margaret," Pete whispered, "listen to the steady, rhythmic patter of moisture dripping to the moss-covered ground. Can you hear it?" he asked. "Can you hear the rustle as the wind sweeps through the branches of the giant fir and hemlock? Can't you just feel the power and sensual essence of the primordial forest? This is my destiny, dear. I feel at peace. These sounds and sights and smells seem like an integral part of my life-force. Listen to the birds, Margaret," Pete rambled on. "Just listen to the manly warble of the split-beaked, clipped-winged, yellow-eyed, snake snorter.

"The songs of these birds clearly signify mother nature's celebration of manliness and the environmental kingdom as it exists in true harmony with the essence of the universe. I can empathize with the gray-billed, wrinkle-faced, wilted-winged, seed sucker as it flies from flower to flower sucking seeds.

From high atop the pines I can hear the high-pitched, naked squeal of the red-faced, bare-ended, thistle-headed, fish flasher.

"The melodic twitter of the three-eyed, bent-beaked, cluster-feathered, fern flapper resonates through the valley. I feel that I am one with nature. I can truly sense a growing brotherhood with the creatures of the earth. I have often dreamed of standing in the dense forest wearing nothing but a loin cloth of leaves. I would carry a twelve-inch blade strapped to my . . ."

"Pete."

"Yes, dear?"

"Shut up!"

Margaret slowly unwrapped a ham sandwich and handed it to Pete. She twisted the cap from the thermos and poured a cup of hot soup into the plastic lid.

"Would you like some crackers with this, dear?"

There was no answer.

"Pete! Do you or don't you want crackers with this?"

"Quiet!"

"Don't tell me to be quiet or I'll lay this soup upside your . . . "

Pete placed his hand over Margaret's mouth.

"Hush, and don't move!"

Pete lifted his hand and pointed to a small group of bushes in front of them.

"There," he whispered, "it's coming through the bushes!"

Margaret's eyes widened and her mouth fell open. Less than fifty feet away stood an eight-hundred-pound black bear. The creature measured a good four feet from forepaw to shoulder with razor-sharp claws and a mouth full of teeth that could easily rip flesh. Pete's eyes squinted and the hair bristled on the back of his neck.

"Be calm, dear!" Pete ordered. "I have prepared for this my entire life. I have always known that my true calling was to be *one with nature*. Like the pioneers and frontiersman, I am physically and mentally prepared to handle any situation regardless of the danger."

The bear raised up on its hind legs. It stood over eleven feet tall. The bear's head twisted left and right, teeth gnashed, and two-inch-long claws ripped through the air as the creature's arms waved wildly at the intruders.

"It will be all right, dear. I'll just yell and wave my arms around and I'm sure the bear will run away. Bears, you see, are nothing but dumb animals. They will only attack humans when they feel that their life is threatened."

Pete flung his arms about wildly while screaming at the top of his lungs. The bear growled and moved closer.

"Oh, my GGGod," Pete stuttered. "OKAY, OKAY! Ah, what we got here is a bluff and, ah, this animal is obviously bluffing and stuff. Yeah, that's it, he's bluffing."

The bear was now within ten feet. Digestive juices were dripping from its massive mandibles. Its eyes were narrow and clearly focused on Pete's throat.

"Oh, dear Lord. Margaret, what am I going to do?"

Margaret took a sip from the cup of soup, wrapped the sandwich in plastic wrap, folded the wax paper back over the crackers, and placed her hand on Pete's leg.

"Start the car, dear. Just roll up the window and start the car."

Bar Wars

EVERY MAN MUST, AT SOME TIME IN HIS LIFE, FIGHT THE dreaded bar wars. I'm not talking about passing the bar exam, nor am I referring to those Friday night binges at the local pub where you sit alone, consume copious amounts of hard liquor, and then somehow believe that you have become attractive to members of the opposite sex. No, this is significantly more socially relevant than lawsuits and booze.

I am talking about a two-foot-long piece of one-inch-square, rectangular plastic. You know, the one that gets put on the conveyor belt between your stuff and their stuff in the grocery store. I am talking about bar wars, the conflict in the rubber zone. The not-so-subtle, psychological disharmony that occurs between normally friendly people when they stand face to face in the check-out line and go to war over the placement of the bar.

The bar is as essential to the integrity of a man's manliness as peeing on a bush is to the integrity of a dog's dogliness. The bar is about the staking of claims and the protection of your space. The bar is not concerned with size or strength or right or wrong. The bar denotes the marking of territory. Like the Berlin wall, it has become a symbolic use of the barrier.

History is full of conflicts that were initiated by one party ignoring the importance of the other party's territorial boundary. Countries have been destroyed for forgetting the basic premise of "this is my space and that is your space." This is very serious business. I have seen a four-pound poodle tear up the leg of a German shepherd that had mistakenly crossed his pee line. There is no room for negotiation. There is no Geneva Convention. There are no prisoners. There is only bite, bite, bite. Bad things are sure to happen.

Someone will carefully place his bar in front of his bag of groceries one day and some fool will violate his space. Instead of reacting calmly and rationally, the offended party will go postal on the aggressor and attack with a relentless barrage of tossed canned goods. I'm not sure that society is ready to deal with having their loved ones bopped upside the head with cans of extra-hot chili.

I have witnessed a little old woman whack a two-hundred-fifty-pound man across the back of the hand with her cane because he had put his beer on her side of the bar. The checkout gal at Fred Meyer reports that a tall, skinny man comes in every morning when the store opens. He puts one stick on each side of his groceries even when no one else is in line, and then he guards his possessions with a ten-ounce can of peas. I have witnessed ordinary people resort to using the bar even when there is three feet of black rubber between their stuff and their enemy's stuff. Some people will spend twenty to thirty seconds just making sure that their bar is equal distance from each side of the belt and perpendicular to the centerline.

The emotions unleashed by bar war skirmishes run the gamut from line rage to paranoid schizophrenia. What if one of their things rolls over the bar into my space and something of mine gets mixed up with something of theirs? I don't want someone I don't even know mixing their stuff up with my stuff. Am I gonna have to pay for their stuff? What if they decide that my stuff is better than their stuff and they try to keep it? Should I put my canned products in the back so I don't lose access to my artillery? Should I buy bigger canned products? Some people have even assumed the role of war monger by becoming supermarket antagonists. They actually go from market to market and initiate bloody, can-throwing conflicts by reaching down and taking the bar away.

People were once civil in grocery stores. They would say hi to each other in the aisles. They would offer to let another shopper go first in line or even help carry bags out to the car. What happened? How has civilization degenerated into this disgusting spectacle that has seemingly materialized right before our unbelieving eyes? I have racked my brain for answers. I have discussed the issue with doctors, scientists and clergymen. There appears to be no solution. There appears to be no logic. Mark my words, the way this thing is degenerating there will eventually be fatalities. Why can't we all just get along?

Spruced Goosed

JEFF WOKE TO FIND HIS WIFE PATTY SITTING AT THE KITCHEN table staring into the front yard.

"What's up, dear?" he inquired.

"Oh," she sighed, "I'm really worried about that nasty old tree out front. I'm concerned that it might fall on the house next time there's a good breeze. I was thinking about calling my dad to have it cut down."

Some women have discovered how incredibly effective it is to play their husbands against their fathers. I don't know why we get so competitive when faced with *daddy competition*, but I'm sure that it's some Freudian thing.

"I can do it!" Jeff protested. "You don't need your dad. I can cut down a stupid ol' tree!"

Jeff collected his supplies from the garage and staged them at the base of the tree. He called for Patty to come out and watch. The need to show off for one's woman is, and always will be, a testosterone thing. Jeff placed a coil of half-inch rope between his teeth, climbed about twenty feet up the tree, made three complete wraps around the trunk, and flashed a manly grin to his woman standing below.

"This oughta hold her, babe," he proudly exclaimed. "I've

secured the end of the rope with a special, double half-hitch, granny knot."

Patty quickly placed her hand over her mouth and managed to subdue the laugh instinct with two forced but credible coughs. Jeff climbed down, placed both thumbs in his belt above each front pocket and slowly walked back and forth in front of the tree. Patty was weakening. It was either laughter or sarcasm but she could be silent no longer.

"Are you going to line dance or cut down the tree, dear? My daddy would have had it split and stacked already."

"Very funny!" he shot back. "You just don't seem to understand how serious this is. Every little thing has got to be just right."

Jeff walked to the far side of the yard, shaded his eyes, and gazed up and down the entire height of the tree.

He looked to the left and then to the right. He stuck his index finger in his mouth and thrust it in the air. His forehead creased deep with thought as he rubbed his chin with his right thumb and forefinger.

"Right here!" he proclaimed, pointing to a one-inch square area in the grass. "I'm gonna lay this baby right here!"

Patty could no longer contain herself.

"Can you tell exactly where it's going to fall just by drooling all over your finger and holding it in the air?"

"No, of course not," Jeff sputtered. "It's all a matter of wind velocity, humidity and barometric pressure and stuff. It's kinda hard to explain unless you know a little about physics. Now stand back and I'll show ya how this is done." Jeff fired up the chain saw and cut about half way through the base of the trunk.

"Okay," he instructed, "I'm gonna wrap the loose end of this rope around my arm and pull it tight. I want you to take the hatchet and start chopping on the other side of the cut I made. When the tree starts to fall, I will pull on the rope and guide it to a pinpoint landing."

"Oh, honey," Patty cooed, "are you sure?"

On the surface and to the untrained ear, this would appear to be a sincere plea by the gentler sex for manly reassurance. However, in spite of the innocent tone and concerned facial expressions, I have found this particular phrase is almost always employed by the female of the species to not only question the manly wisdom of a particular course of action but to pass feminine summary judgment on the entire male decision-making process. Jeff, unfortunately, had an untrained ear.

"Don't worry, baby," he condescended, "I know what I'm doing."

You would think at that point, if the woman really loved him, she'd wipe the smirk off her face and just come right out and tell him he was being an idiot. I guess some things are just too good to pass up. The nearest neighbor, who taught mathematics at the junior high school and was watching the entertainment out the kitchen window, estimated Jeff's trajectory to be about forty-five degrees, with the apex of his flight a good twenty feet off the ground.

The tree cleanly missed the house and landed about three inches in front of the windshield wipers on Jeff's new car.

Jeff expressed his concerns immediately upon awakening in the emergency room, "What happened? Did the tree land where I said it would? Is my car okay?"

"You get some rest and don't worry your pretty little head about a thing, dear," Patty assured him. "I called Daddy and he said he would come over and fix everything."

I find it astounding how fragile manliness can be. One well-timed, derisive criticism from virtually any female can instantaneously peel away the delicate facade of any man's manliness.

Hard To Digest

I HAVE BEEN A WORKING MAN FOR MOST OF MY LIFE. FOR OVER thirty years I have toiled for the boss. I have walked his walk. I have talked his talk. I have lifted his barge and I have toted his bale. He even got me out on bail a couple of times. But now it is over. I will no longer slave away in obscurity. I will no longer scratch out a meager existence and live precariously from check to check. Overdrafts, tax penalties and second mortgage payments are a thing of the past. Starting whistles, lunch hours, and vacation leave are history. I will soon be my own man. I will owe no taskmaster my obedience. I will be the manliest of men. I will be a man with cash.

I probably shouldn't be telling you about this, but I opened my mail five months ago and my entire life was instantly changed. There in my hand was my salvation, the answer to all of my dreams. I was somehow miraculously selected as a finalist in the Sweepstakes, and I was holding, as proof, a Grand Prize Eligibility Notice complete with a lawyer-certified, printed parchment informing me that I may have already won a large sum of cash. Now granted it was only the preliminary stage but I was guaranteed, in writing, the opportunity to win. I also received a bonus sticker good for a new automobile plus an extra cash dividend for early submittal.

Since that initial surprise, I have received more and more information. Four months ago I was notified in a special certified envelope that I had been accepted into the Secondary Stage of the contest. I was ensured that, as a Second Stage finalist, additional money had been earmarked for placement into the prestigious and highly touted Business Bank of Connecticut as soon as my victory was confirmed. I know this sounds too good to be true, but the postman repeatedly visited me in the following months serving to further solidify my position. I have received acceptance to the Primary Stage, the Final Stage, the Super Final Stage, and the Final Elimination Round. Yesterday I was delivered a large brown envelope. My

name was printed in bold black letters and clearly visible through the plastic window.

I made it! This is it! I am a finalist in the Super Bonus Round. The check has been cut and is awaiting deposit into an account specially opened in my name. I'm talking seven figures here. Do you want to know the really exciting part about this miraculous windfall? I'm about to become independently wealthy, and I did it all for the meager cost of only four magazine subscriptions!

Building Character

I HAD A PAPER ROUTE WHEN I WAS A KID. I DIDN'T WANT A paper route. I hated paper routes. My old man told me to get a paper route because paper routes build character. I delivered the morning paper in a place called Bremerton Gardens. I would wake up at 4:00 and walk over five miles in the rain, sleet, snow and dark so people I didn't know could read the news while they ate their breakfast. Once a month I would walk around in the evening in the rain, sleet, snow and dark to collect money from people I didn't know who would yell at me because their paper got wet on the third Thursday of the month or because I missed them altogether.

Bremerton Gardens was essentially an apartment complex. There were numerous huge buildings. Each building contained eight dwellings. The complex was separated east from west by a deep ravine. A long wooden bridge connected the two sides and a chain link fence ran north and south along the bank to prevent people from tumbling in.

One spring day I was halfway through my morning ritual when I was overcome by the physical desire to perform a critical biological function. I was a good three miles from my house and I had to go to the bathroom. Now normally one can delay these things until the location is more appropriate. In this case, the urge was painfully overwhelming. Fortunately, I was delivering papers so the problem of cleaning up after performing the function was not a primary concern.

Though it was dark, I was worried that someone might see me, so I crawled down over the embankment and stood a few feet from the fence facing uphill. I lowered my pants and assumed the squat. I did my duty, which was a great relief. Unbeknownst to me, the entire business had selected the crotch of my jeans as its final resting place. When I pulled my pants up, the resulting pressurized explosion of processed food products was unmerciful in its rapid and random distribution. I do believe that particular three-mile walk home was the longest and squishiest of my life.

My mother was cooking breakfast when I waddled through the back door. "My Lord, child, what in God's name happened to you?"

"No big deal, Mom, nothing to worry about, I'm just *building character.*"

Malled To Death

CHRISTMAS WAS COMING UP QUICK. THIS WAS THE TIME OF year that strikes fear into the hearts of men. Men everywhere cringe at the very thought of those well-worn words leaving the lips of their women. "Dear," it usually begins, "let's go to the Mall and go shopping."

Now there are numerous patented manly responses to this extremely frightening request. The most common are designed to fend off the inevitable for as long as possible, such as "Huh?"—which is used to feign deafness. There is also the ever-popular question approach, "Ah, did you want to go right this very minute?" Or, the seldom used and pitifully ineffective primordial response of "Nooooooooooooooooooo!"

Real men of course simply tell their women that they have absolutely no intention of being dragged down to the Mall or any other place to go shopping. I've never met any of these men, but I know they're out there somewhere.

Women, apparently, do not seem to understand the real problem men have with the whole concept of shopping, This is not surprising since these same women are also unable to fathom why many men would rather die than dance.

I intend to use this text to finally set the record straight.

First of all, men do not hate going to the Mall to buy something. I know that sounds one hundred and eighty degrees
out from where this story was headed but it's really just a
question of semantics. Men don't dislike buying; they just
abhor shopping. I go to the Mall and buy things regularly.
Just yesterday I drove to the Mall, pulled around to the east
entrance where the front door of J.C. Penney's is clearly
marked, parked in the closest available spot, walked in, went
right to the jeans section, grabbed a pair of 33 x 34 Levi's,
paid for them, and got the heck outta there. Total time: four
minutes, thirty-seven seconds. That's kinda slow but there
were women shopping everywhere and I was trying to keep
from getting in their way.

I am also not immune to impulse shopping. If something
catches my eye while I'm running to the jeans section or

while I'm escaping via the shortest route, I have been known to grab it on the run and pay for it at the register closest to the exit. Men of course will always have time to look at "men things" to buy, but you must note that they do not shop for these things. They scope them out and buy them.

I have seen my wife shop for six hours and not buy anything. How does that work? It's scary. They make us go with them. Helpless and subdued men are subjected to the terrors of the jungle in their own backyards. Men face being torn to shreds by wild-eyed women at Wonder Bra sales. Men are verbally abused by hormone-packing adolescents prowling the halls in roving gangs. Men are subjected to crying babies, Mall food poisoning, and bathrooms that can't be found. Men are left standing in the middle of lingerie departments not knowing where to direct their eyes. Men are forced to wait while their wives try on thirty-seven outfits without buying anything. They are then requested to respond to rapid-fire questions that have only one possible answer: "Do I look good in this, dear? Does it make me look fat?"

It is really all too frightening. True manliness demands that buying something consists of four distinct operational phases: the target, the rendezvous, the assault and the escape. I realize there is a certain military slant to this buying technique, but you see, to a man, shopping is a combat situation and the deep-seated fear of even the manliest of men is being caught in the middle of a shopping frenzy and getting *Malled* to death.

Image

REALITY ASIDE, THERE ARE FEW THINGS MORE IMPORTANT than image. Basketball players with misplaced jewelry and multicolored hair are crafting an image. Hollywood stars with expensive Jaguars make money because of their image. Chief Executive Officers of billion-dollar, multi-national conglomerates are well aware of the importance of their image. You have an image, I have an image, everyone has an image. Our image determines how we are perceived, as well as how people react and respond.

Based on the above-mentioned, well-worded, but faulty premise, I feel that our peace officers are walkin' around packin' the wrong image. When I think of cops, I think of clean, polished, brass-buttoned, public servants who have placed our safety and protection above all other things. I see conscientious officers obtaining search warrants and reading Miranda to offenders to avoid violating our civil rights. I see flag-carrying men of the law escorting our young, innocent, school children across auto-infested thoroughfares. I see clean, loyal, brave, reverent . . . well anyway, you get the drift.

I'm not sure the status quo is all that effective at actually deterring criminal behavior. I have always believed that cops would be far more effective if they modified their image. Good traffic cops, for example, should be, at a minimum, six-foot-four and two-hundred-fifty pounds of solid muscle. The men should be even bigger! They should have beards and greasy, long hair. They should wear leather jackets with a pig's skull and crossbones on the back, and they should ride Harleys and carry UZIs. When a cop pulls you over for a moving violation, the absolute last thing on your mind should be giving him any lip. Everything about his posture, appearance and etiquette should demand immediate and unconditional respect.

"Yo, dirtbag, ya got even the vaguest idea why I pulled ya over instead of just blowing your worthless carcass away, or am I gonna have to drag your wimpy butt outta that vehicle and make ya a messy roadside example?"

"No, Mr. Officer, Sir. I understand I was exceeding the speed limit. I know I was tailgating and failed to follow the vehicle in front of me at the proper distance under existing weather conditions. I am also more than cognizant of my failure to yield the right of way back there at that four-way stop. If you could find forgiveness in your heart, I swear on a stack of bibles that I will be forever in your debt, and I promise on my mother's eyes that I will never, ever do it again."

"Make sure ya don't, meat! I'm gonna give ya a ticket for speeding and I'm gonna confiscate your vehicle. Pay the ticket by next Tuesday or I'll hunt ya down and permanently terminate your retirement options. If I ever again catch ya going as much as one mile an hour over the speed limit, I'll hit ya so hard the echo will come back and break both your ankles.

Ya got a problem with any of this?"

"No, Sir. I understand your need to respond to my indiscretions in this appropriately forceful manner and I again apologize for causing you any difficulty."

I have always maintained that this simple, fundamental change in the image of our Men in Blue would drastically reduce, if not eliminate, burglary, speeding, domestic disputes, driving under the influence, muggings, going slow in the fast lane, shoplifting, turning without signaling, and road rage.

I have just recently, however, found a large number of detractors to my theory. Strangely, there seem to be groups of people in densely populated urban areas who are now telling me police officers have utilized certain aspects of my proposed modified image for years with apparent impunity, and with very little noticeable reduction in crime. So, never mind!

GLM

COACHES FROM RIVAL BALL CLUBS GATHER ON THE MUDDY field, clipboards in hand. Hundreds of young kids laugh and giggle. Parents huddle in small groups discussing work and weather. Baseballs fly in all directions. This is Little League draft day. Each year, at this time, youngsters are separated by age and given the opportunity to demonstrate their natural baseball ability. Each child is tested and rated in three basic skill areas: catching ground balls, shagging pop flies, and knocking the cover off the ball. Numeric ratings from one to ten are used to note a child's ability in each attribute. One's, two's and three's are common. A ten rating is very rare and only given to a kid with great future marketing potential.

Dave had been a Little League coach for four years. In the world of Little League coaching, four years is an eternity. Arguing with protective parents and stubborn umpires aside, draft day was his favorite time. He held the bottom of his clipboard against his stomach and marked special notes to the right of each kid's name. The notes were invaluable when it came time to make draft selections.

Dave noticed a young man with a clipboard standing to his right. Like Dave, the man was marking special notes. Dave

casually moved closer until he was slightly behind and to the left of his competitor. He could read the young man's notes over his shoulder. The first kid on the list was rated a four and the words *good arm. Possible pitcher* were scribbled in the right-hand margin. Dave looked at his notes. He had made a similar comment.

The notes on the second kid said *backs off on ground balls, good swing, GLM.* Dave looked at his notes. He had also noted solid batting mechanics and a problem with fielding ground balls.

The notes on the third kid said *good hand-eye coordination, GLM.*

Dave systematically compared notes on each kid. However,

every third or fourth entry included the note GLM. Dave was embarrassed that he didn't recognize the meaning of the term. Was it Good Lively Mitt? Was it Glove Movement? This was important stuff! The competitive pressure was too much. Dave had to know what the mysterious rating meant.

Dave wandered around the field and asked thirteen other coaches the meaning of GLM. Not one had the answer. There was only one solution. He had to ask the young man.

"Excuse me, I, ah, noticed that you're a coach."

"Yes," the young man answered, "this is my first year."

"Well," Dave stuttered, "I, ah, accidentally saw your draft notes, and I noticed the term GLM is marked after several players. I guess I was wondering if that means like, ah, Good Lively Mitt or something?"

The young man looked down at his notes and laughed.

"What's so funny?" Dave barked, somewhat embarrassed.

"Well, ya see," the young man said, "ya gotta understand. I'm a single guy and GLM stands for Good Lookin' Mom."

Water World

MY WIFE LYNNE CONTRIBUTED HER WATERBED TO OUR marriage. Initially, I was very fond of sleeping on a mattress that had its own tidal action. I found it soothing and some-what comforting to be gently rocked on a cushion of waves.

The first sign of trouble was awakening in the middle of the night thinking that I had wet the bed. I was shocked and embarrassed. I thought I had outgrown that humiliating habit in my late twenties. I was, however, innocent. Apparently, waterbeds are not immune to cat kneading. The patch job was relatively easy once I finished spending four or five hours searching for the microscopic claw hole.

The second indication of trouble occurred on the morning we were packing to move to our new house. I was busy load-ing boxes in the truck. Lynne asked if I could give her a hand draining the bed. I have moved a dozen times in my life but I have never had to drain a bed. There were hoses and fixtures and adapters sticking out in all directions. The empty rubber mattress weighed about four thousand pounds, and the two-by-ten bed frame had a heating pad with wires protruding from the corners. When we got it set up in the new bedroom, we had to wait two days for it to warm up before we could sleep in it.

Years have passed. I believe I am now suffering permanent, chronic, debilitating, anatomical afflictions caused by the
waterbed's bone-warping lack of skeletal support. My feet
hurt, my back hurts, my neck hurts, my right arm hurts, and
my left arm regularly goes numb. I can no longer stand up
straight. I find it virtually impossible to turn over in the
middle of the night without pushing on something solid to
gain leverage. I have learned to use the head of my soundly
sleeping wife for this purpose.

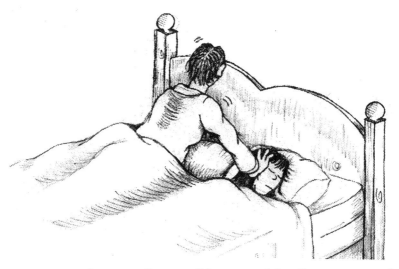

In several years, I fear I will be incapable of getting out of
bed without assistance. I will be in a nursing home before I'm
eligible to retire. I have expressed my concerns to Lynne over
and over again but to no avail. I told her that my feet, back,
neck and arms were in constant pain. My pleas for relief have
been repetitively rebuffed.

The other day I purchased a two-hundred-dollar orthopedic pillow with form-fitting magic foam. The flyer promised

full support for the neck muscles. The next morning I was unable to move my head. I took it back to the store but they wouldn't give me a refund. They said they couldn't accept returned pillows if the purchaser had tried out the product by actually sleeping on it.

I walked around for two weeks in a neck brace, eating instant breakfast through a straw.

Lynne finally showed signs of being sympathetic. She promised to buy me an orthopedic pillow for $9.95. I told her my two-hundred-dollar pillow with special form-fitting magic foam had been entirely ineffective and I couldn't believe a $9.95 pillow could possibly help. She assured me this was a newly designed orthopedic pillow she had personally re-searched on the Internet. She picked out the best of the bunch and was positive this pillow would bring instant relief. She said when I fell asleep that she would put the new $9.95 orthopedic pillow over my face and push down hard until my chest stopped moving. This, she insisted, would solve the entire problem for the both of us. I'm not sure I am receiving the appropriate level of empathy on this issue.

There is hope on the horizon, however. Lynne tells me the newer waterbed mattresses are made with baffles to even out the support and provide a firm and resilient sleeping surface that feels just like a regular bed. I want to know why we can't just buy a regular bed mattress made with coils to even out the support and provide a firm and resilient sleeping surface that feels just like one of the new waterbed mattresses?

The Hunt

THE LEAVES WERE TURNING. FOOTBALL WAS ONCE AGAIN THE number one targeted frequency of remote controls everywhere. Fall had arrived. It was the time of year many men consider to be optimum for partaking in manly adventures, a time to bond and banter with buddies, a time to taunt mother nature, brave the elements, and make that long, tedious, perilous journey back to our roots—back to a past that reverberates with the raw essence of manliness—back to a time when men were men and ships were wood—back to a time when the stealth and cunning of a man was all that stood between starvation and death—back to the hunt.

This was the time for men to drive to whatever was left of the wilderness. This was the time for men to set up camp in a propane-heated recreational vehicle complete with electric lights, running water, indoor plumbing, and quadraphonic stereo.

This was a time for men to stay up late at night and share stories of previous conquests. This was a time for men to consume copious amounts of hard liquor. This was a time for men to venture out into the beckoning wilderness and stand face to face with wild game—armed with nothing more than a

tiny little rifle that fires harmless lead projectiles at a muzzle velocity of over 3500 feet per second. This was the time for men to be real men . . . and kill something. This was hunting season. It was also an excellent time for some men to leave the little women at home and stalk the most elusive prey of all, the two-legged kind.

Andy had it all figured out. "I'll tell the wife I'm going hunting," he thought to himself. "I'll tell her I'm going to Blue Mountain like I always do, and then I'll set up camp like I always do. I'll drive down to Mooseville like I always do, hang around in Bucks Inn like I always do, and see if I can score."

Andy fancied himself a killer with the ladies. He had spent many a hunting trip rejuvenating some of his most successful pre-marital pickup lines. There was the somewhat trite but always powerful: "Hi, sugar lips, wanna mess around?" And

of course, the killer line that Andy claimed never failed him:
"Hey, baby, can I buy you a drink and stuff?"

Andy and the boys arrived at their favorite camping spot
around 6:30 on the first evening of their five-day trip. The
journey to the mountain had been long and humid. Andy
was hot and sweaty and decided a quick shower would be
imperative if he was going to nab him a babe. Andy quickly
dried himself off and dug through his pack in search of clean
clothes. There were socks, pants, and shirts but no clean underwear.

"Hey, guys, can I borrow a pair of somebody's clean underwear?" The boys responded in silent unison. "Come on,
you guys," Andy pleaded, "I can't go into town without clean
underwear." Joe was the only buddy to respond. "What's

wrong with you, man. Are you nuts? Forget it! What if the guys back at the office found out we shared underwear?"

Andy pulled on his crusty skivvies and finished dressing. At 8:35 Andy and the boys headed down Blue Mountain into Mooseville for an unscheduled rendezvous with the beautiful bimbos of Bucks Inn.

Night after night they repeated their journey. Shower after shower Andy's already thin chances of scoring with a babe got thinner and thinner as his skivvies got crustier and crustier.

Andy sat in silence on the way home. His mind was busy formulating tales of wild animals and wilderness survival. He smiled as he envisioned his wife sitting in silent reverence, awed by his carefully crafted stories of skill and cunning. Andy waved to the boys, slung his rifle over his shoulder, and reached for the door handle. His wife opened the door.

"Hi, my pet," she cooed, "how is my big, strong, hunting man? How was your trip? Did you have fun in the woods with your friends?" Andy's chest swelled with manly pride. "You bet, darlin', we had ourselves a swell time. Did ya miss me?"

"I missed you so much I could hardly sleep. I laid in bed for hours and hours every single night you were away from me worried that you might be hurt, or lost, or in some horrible danger, and I wondered how I could ever possibly go on with my life should anything happen to my man."

Andy's eyes narrowed, his throat tightened, and tiny beads of perspiration began forming on his forehead. She's laying this on a bit thick he thought to himself. He forced a hesitant response. "I'm sorry you worried, hon, but I'm . . . a . . . back now and it's . . . a . . . all gonna be. . . ."

She continued as if he had never opened his mouth: "I really was distraught when my cousin Thelma from Mooseville called to say she thought she saw you at a tavern. I told her it couldn't possibly be you, not my husband, but she insisted that she saw someone that looked like you and a bunch of your stinking buddies lurking around Bucks Inn trying to get your antlers trimmed! She said that if you were half the man your dog thought you were then I should be worried."

"Listen, woman," Andy stammered, "we were up at the crack a dawn every single day. We slung our rifles over our shoulders and struggled through waist-deep snow just to bring home fresh meat. I was workin' my butt off tryin' to provide sustenance for my loved ones, and what kinda gratitude do I get from you? You accuse me of . . . a . . . antler stuff and a . . . you didn't even bother to pack me any underwear!"

"I'm so sorry, dear," she placated with a fringe of sarcasm, "I really do appreciate your efforts to bring home the bacon. I suspect that my cousin Thelma was probably just drinkin' a bit too much. Sometimes she imagines things that aren't really there. I'm glad you're home and I'm happy that you had a good time with your pals. I have dinner on the table and a fire in the fireplace, and oh, by the way, I did pack you some clean underwear. I put them in your rifle case."

V-her-bal Essence

I AM A WHITE MALE AND, CONSEQUENTLY, I AM LABELED AS being born to power and privilege. I can live with that stereotype. I am not, however, insensitive to the cultural and gender inequities that surround us all. I am a proponent of equal opportunity. I firmly believe that the labor force should be as diverse as the population it employs. What I'm not in favor of is what I perceive as a plot by women to systematically immasculate men. Before you accuse me of steppin' off the deep end, please let me explain the premise for my accusation.

The most powerful man in history was reported to be Hercules. So what's with the name? Shouldn't it have been His-cules? Do you see what I mean? There is obviously a Delilah in the works here somewhere. How else would you explain the manliest of men being named Her-cules? This whole thing is all a sinister plot.

The more I analyze it the angrier I

get. Think about it. Female babies learn to talk months before male babies. I'm positive they have been taking advantage of the head start. Somebody recently decided to name tropical storms after men. No problem, right? Then why are these storms still referred to as her-icanes? What's wrong with him-icanes? Look in the dictionary. It's all right there in black and white.

Many of the dinosaurs were her-bivores. Yet half of them were males. Men who own and breed livestock are referred to as her-dsmen. All of our physical and mental attributes are attributed to her-edity. I can't even go fishing without using her-ring. If you save a bunch of people from a burning building do they call you a him-ro? No. If you try to escape it all by moving out into the deep woods, do they call you a him-mit? No. When you die, do you go to the him-after? Absolutely not. Have you ever heard of a man lifting something that was too heavy and getting a him-nia? No, no, no!

Fortunately, men, there are still a few remaining examples of how things should really be. Women are still known for getting his-terical, and they are sometimes required to have his-torectomies. The entire documented record of humanity is rightfully referred to as his-tory. These few things stand as reassuring bastions of manliness. However, even they are under subtle attack. When you get a cold, do you take an anti-his-tamine? You would think this is good because it is a his-tamine, but if it's an anti-his-tamine isn't that the first step to becoming a her-stamine?

Look, I don't want to stir up any trouble. I just want all of you men to be aware of the direction of the attack. I want you all to be cognizant of the subtlety of the plan. We are under siege. First the language, and then football! Once I have made all men aware, I believe we will be able to clear that first herdle and achieve an inevitable victory.

Totally Pipular II

DAVE'S WIFE ANITA WAS WORRIED TO DEATH ABOUT THE PIPES in the garage. The weather had turned cold, and she had heard too many horror stories of pipes freezing and then breaking and flooding the house.

"Dear," she cooed, as they lay in bed that night, "could you please do something with the pipes in the garage so they don't freeze and break and flood the house?"

"Pipes," Dave mumbled, half asleep, "what pipes?"

"The pipes in the garage, dear. I'm really afraid they might freeze and break."

"Look, dear," Dave reasoned, "we've lived here fourteen years now and we've never, ever, had problems with the pipes freezing. Now, go to sleep."

Dave sat at the breakfast table the next morning. Anita stood at the kitchen window staring at the thick layer of frost on the lawn.

"Dave," she pleaded, "the thermometer outside shows eighteen degrees. I'm really concerned about the pipes freezing and breaking and flooding the house."

"Anita," Dave smoothed, "in 1992 the temperature was seventeen degrees and the pipes in the garage did not freeze.

Everything will be just fine, okay?"

"Well, okay, dear, if you say so."

Dave smiled, gave her a hug and a quick kiss, and headed out the door to work. At 12:30 that afternoon the phone rang. It was Anita.

"David," she snapped, "the temperature has gone down to sixteen degrees and if those pipes freeze I am going to be very upset!"

"Calm down, dear," a slight hint of irritation coloring his tone. "The pipes are not going to freeze. If you insist on being concerned about the pipes, then I'll stop by the hardware store on the way home and pick up the materials I'll need to wrap them up. Okay? I have to go now. There's someone in my office."

Dave let go of the receiver about one inch above its resting place. There was a distinct thud as it fell into place. The visitor couldn't help but notice Dave's anxiety.

"What's the problem, old buddy?" he inquired.

"Oh, it's no big deal," Dave mumbled. "My wife is concerned about the pipes freezing, and she keeps buggin' me about wrapping them up."

The visitor asked Dave if the pipes were outside. Dave told him they were in the garage.

"That's not a problem," the visitor explained. "You simply have to open the door from the kitchen area into the garage. The warmth from the house will keep the garage warm enough to prevent the pipes from freezing. I do it all the time. Works great! Give your wife a call and you can solve this whole mess."

Dave was elated. When his visitor left, Dave called Anita and gave her the good news. "Open up the door to the garage, dear, and let a little heat get in there. That'll warm them pipes up."

After work the vanpool vehicle turned the corner and headed down Dave and Anita's street. Dave had had a long, hard day and was looking forward to a good dinner and a restful evening. He looked up the driveway in disbelief. There was nothing to do but laugh. His car, his tools, and all of the pipes were covered in wind-swept snow. The garage door was wide open!

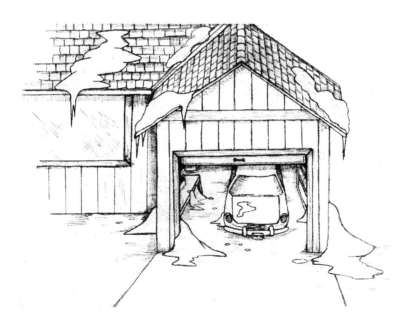

Carpe Diem

A VERY CLOSE FRIEND OF MINE WROTE A SONG WHEN HE WAS fifteen years old. The lyrics are rather puerile, but they seem very profound as I reach middle ground.

> Time passes by
> when you're not looking that way
> and you will find you've missed it
> when your hair is gray
> and you will know just when
> it's your turn to say
> Time won't stand still
> It won't stop and wait for you
> Time won't stand still
> It has no debts to pay

I will be fifty years old, or young, depending on who's doing the reading, on the 27th of December 1999. That's five decades, one half of a century, five percent of a millennium. I want to know how this has happened! I want to know how I got here so fast! It's not that I'm particularly upset about the way things have gone. In between disasters I've had some very interesting experiences. What startles me is the realization of just how short fifty years is. It's nothing! It is a flash in the pan.

Five hundred years ago is a mere pittance. I've lived ten percent of myself. I try to remember the wisdom of sages from so many ages: You only go around once in life. Take time to smell the roses. Live one day at a time. Today is the first day of the rest of your life. Carpe Diem, seize the day!

Danny and I wish each of you many manly adventures, and please remember two things:

Time won't stand still; it won't stop and wait for you.

Time won't stand still; it has no debts to pay.

And we find it astounding how fragile manliness can be. One well-timed, derisive criticism from virtually any female can instantaneously peel away the delicate facade of any man's manliness.